OCEANS

The Vast, Mysterious Deep

by David L. Harrison

Illustrated by Cheryl Nathan

Boyds Mills Press

The author wishes to thank Erwin J. Mantei, Ph.D., professor of geology, Southwest Missouri State University, for his review of the original manuscript.

Published by Boyds Mills Press
A Highlights Company
815 Church Street
Honesdale, Pennsylvania 18431
Printed in China

Publisher Cataloging-in-Publication Data (U.S.)

Harrison, David.
    Oceans : the vast, mysterious deep / by David L. Harrison ;
illustrations by Cheryl Nathan. — 1st ed.
[32] p. : col. ill. ; cm.
Summary: A basic introduction to oceans: how they were formed and
how they work.
ISBN 1-59078-018-3
1. Ocean—Juvenile literature. (1. Ocean.) I. Nathan, Cheryl.
II. Title
577.7 21   2003
2002108412

First edition, 2003
The text of this book is set in 18-point Optima.

Visit our Web site at www.boydsmillspress.com

10 9 8 7 6 5 4 3 2 1

To Sandy Asher, good friend for so many reasons
—D. L. H.

For Tucker and Katy
—C. N.

The blue whale may weigh
300,000 pounds.
It is the largest animal
that has ever lived,
and it lives in oceans
around the world.

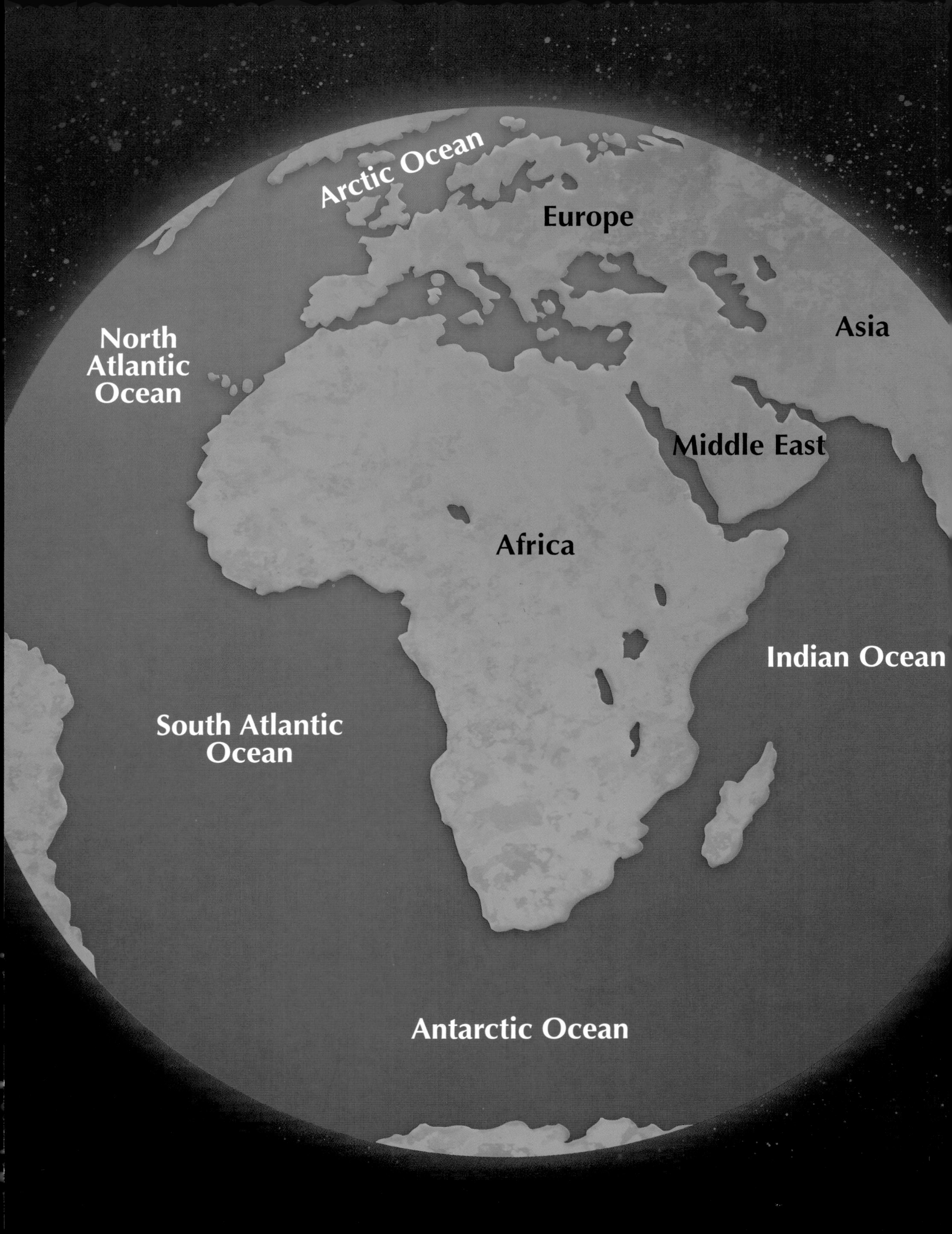
Arctic Ocean
Europe
Asia
North Atlantic Ocean
Middle East
Africa
Indian Ocean
South Atlantic Ocean
Antarctic Ocean

Asia

North Pacific
Ocean

North
America

More than 70 percent
of the earth
is covered by oceans—
the Pacific, Atlantic,
Indian, Antarctic, and Arctic.
The Pacific is so enormous
that all the land in the world
could fit inside it.
Where did so much water
come from?

South Pacific
Ocean

stralia

Antarctica

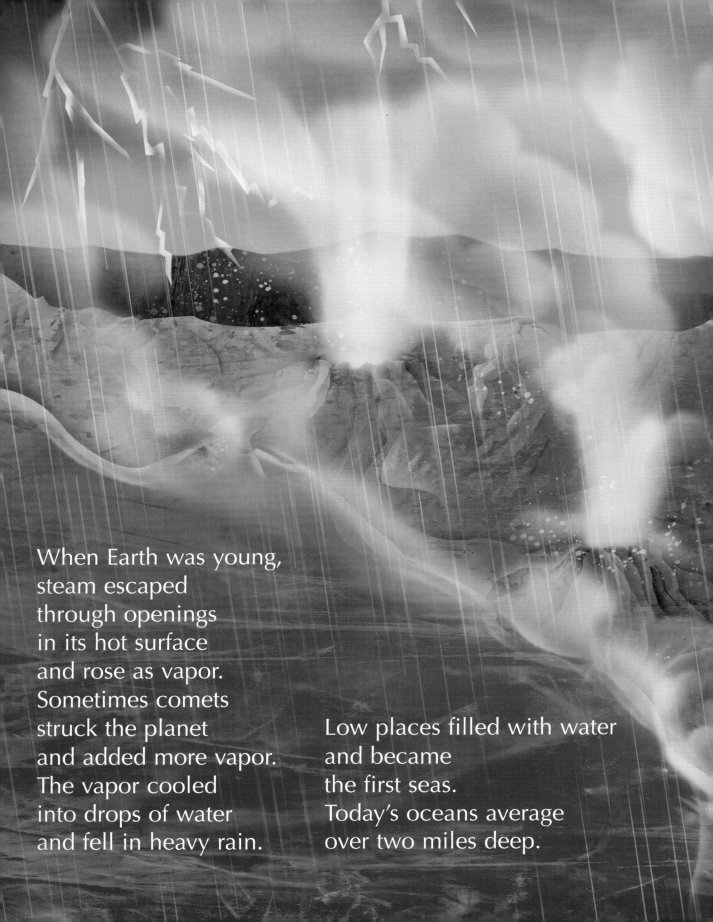

When Earth was young,
steam escaped
through openings
in its hot surface
and rose as vapor.
Sometimes comets
struck the planet
and added more vapor.
The vapor cooled
into drops of water
and fell in heavy rain.

Low places filled with water
and became
the first seas.
Today's oceans average
over two miles deep.

Now the water supply
is used over and over.
Vapor from the ocean
moves in clouds
and falls from the sky
as rain or snow.
Most water that reaches land
flows downhill in rivers
or under the ground
and finally returns to the sea.
Salt from soil and rocks
turns the seawater salty.

The ocean shelf
leads out from shore.
More plants and animals
live there than anywhere else
in the ocean.
Around the world
people depend on
tuna, cod, herring,
shrimp, crabs, lobsters,
and other creatures
living there by the millions.

Moray
eel

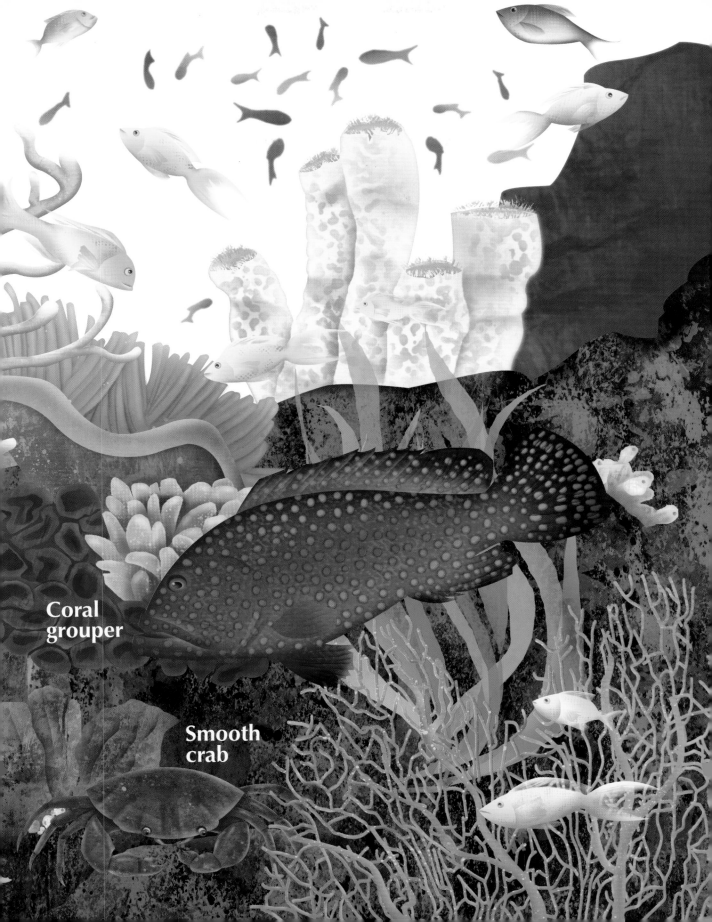

Coral grouper

Smooth crab

Farther out,
beyond the shelf,
lies the deep black bottom
of the sea.
Much of it is flat
and covered by sandy mud.
Without sunlight,
plants cannot grow.
The pressure above
from so much water
would squash most creatures.

Nevertheless, animals do
live on the bottom—
strange animals
that eat one another
or search the ooze
for crumbs that settle there.

Gulper eel

Anglerfish

Lantern fish

Tripod fish

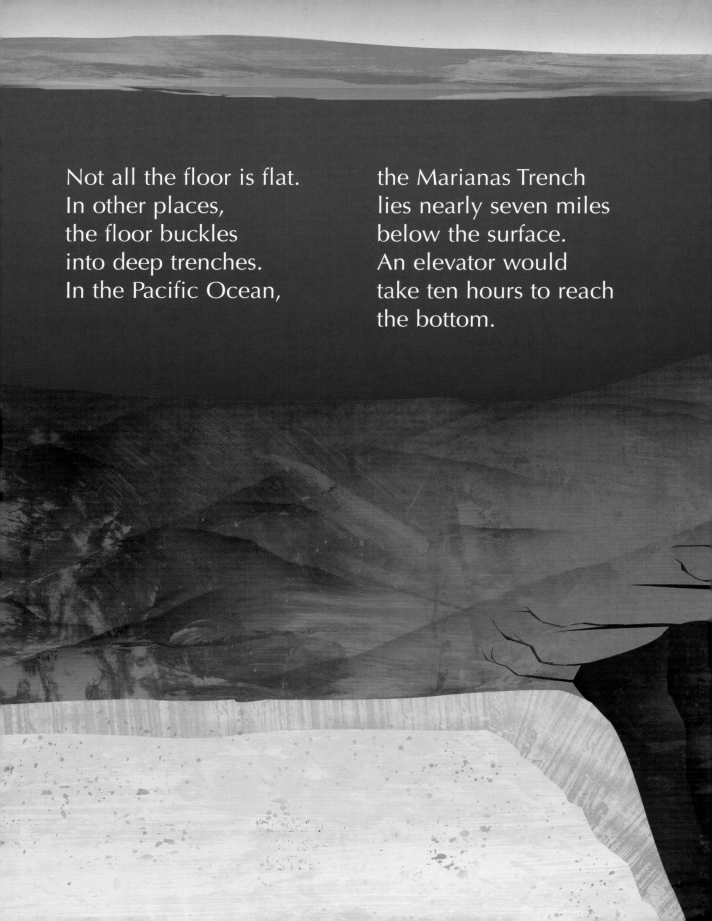

Not all the floor is flat.
In other places,
the floor buckles
into deep trenches.
In the Pacific Ocean,
the Marianas Trench
lies nearly seven miles
below the surface.
An elevator would
take ten hours to reach
the bottom.

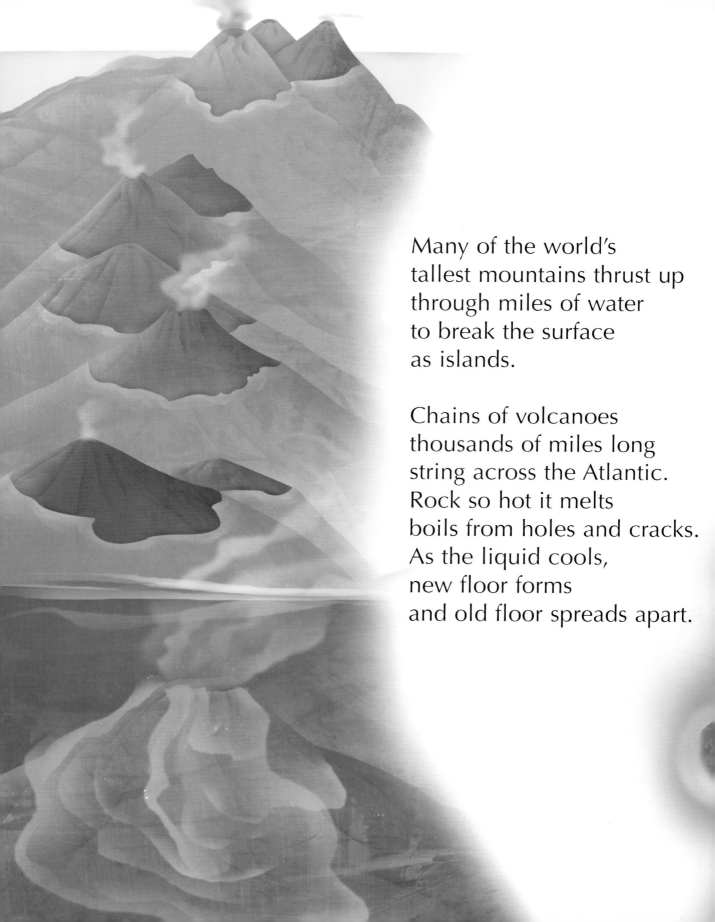

Many of the world's
tallest mountains thrust up
through miles of water
to break the surface
as islands.

Chains of volcanoes
thousands of miles long
string across the Atlantic.
Rock so hot it melts
boils from holes and cracks.
As the liquid cools,
new floor forms
and old floor spreads apart.

When the floor shakes
from earthquakes
or violent volcanoes,
shocks may send long waves
called tsunamis (soo-NAH-mees)
racing across the water
hundreds of miles per hour.
Tsunami waves
cause great harm
crashing into the land.

Normal waves start
with wind across the water.
They begin small,
building as they go.
In warm water,
strong winds make extra vapor
that feeds growing storms.

Some severe storms—
called hurricanes,
typhoons, or cyclones—
grow hundreds of miles wide.
They howl across the water
like tops whirling
150 miles per hour,
throwing waves
100 feet high.

But even in calm weather
the ocean is never still.
Wind on the surface
moves water in currents.
The Gulf Stream current
flows 100 miles
or more per day
like a wide river
across the Atlantic
to the British Isles.

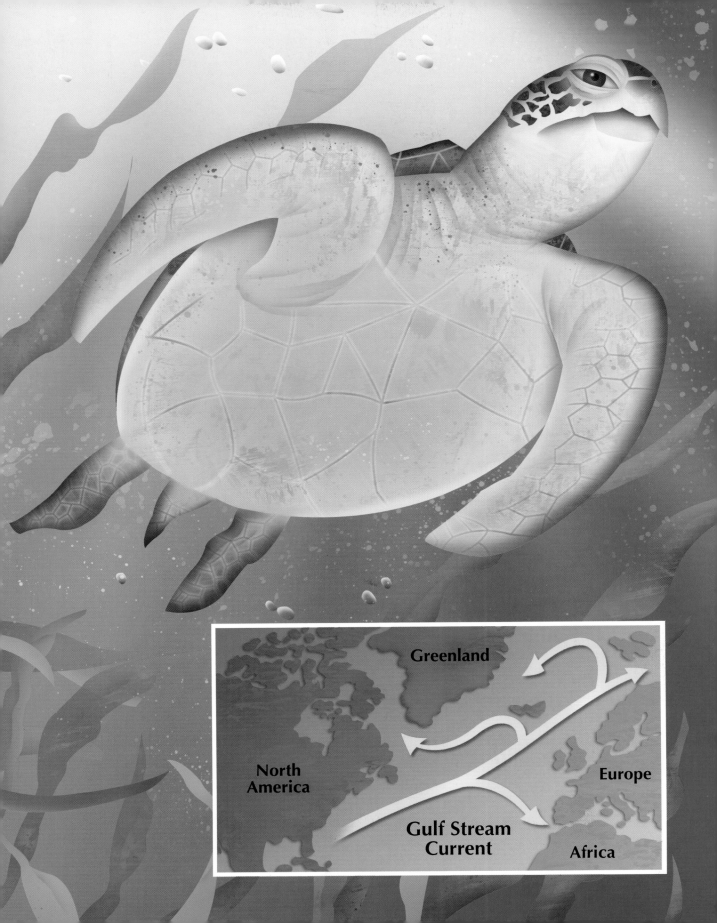

Greenland

North
America

Europe

**Gulf Stream
Current**

Africa

Water gets heavier
when it cools.
In freezing climates,
cold surface water sinks
and creeps along
in deep, slow currents.
In the Arctic Ocean
around the North Pole,
water freezes into ice.
Huge chunks called icebergs
break off and float away.

Glaciers build when
thick layers of snow
pack into ice.
They slide slowly to the sea
and split off as icebergs.
Monsters the size of Rhode Island
can happen near the South Pole
in the Antarctic Ocean.

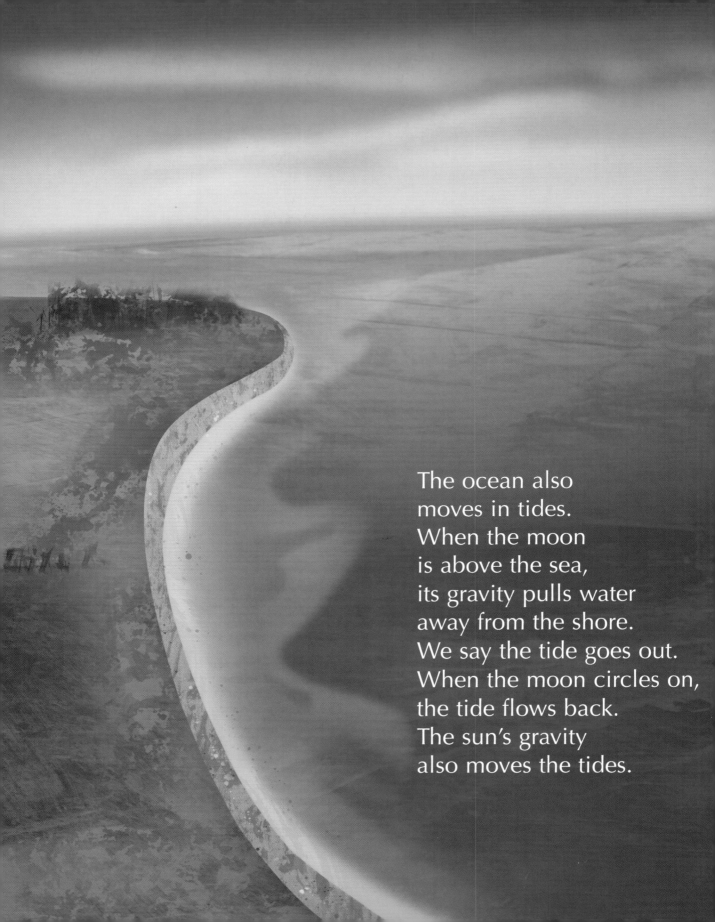

The ocean also
moves in tides.
When the moon
is above the sea,
its gravity pulls water
away from the shore.
We say the tide goes out.
When the moon circles on,
the tide flows back.
The sun's gravity
also moves the tides.

We depend on the ocean.
We travel across it.
Live and play on its shores.
Fish and trap for food.
Gather its pearls.
Take its minerals,
oils, and salt.

But every year
we pollute the ocean
and harm its plants and animals.
We kill dolphins in our nets
and catch so many fish
that some kinds
are lost forever.
Once there were
200,000 blue whales.

Today 5,000 are left.
We must learn
to take better care.
Without the ocean,
our lives could never
be the same.

AUTHOR'S NOTE

Water appeared on Earth even while the young planet was shuddering and cracking open in turmoil from molten rock, volcanic eruptions, and violent storms. The bombardment of comets may have contributed greatly to the growing accumulation of water. And since most of our water supply keeps recycling—from ocean to atmosphere to land and back to ocean—the bath we take tonight may have molecules in it that came from space.

Oceans began so long ago that we cannot know everything about them. Over long periods of time, the slow but steady drift of continents changes the shape and even the location of oceans. Separating Earth's outer crust (where we live) from the mantle below it is a series of gigantic interlocking plates. These tectonic plates move very slowly, carrying all land and oceans on their backs. But when these giants rub against one another, the earth trembles from their mighty force. If the shock occurs in an ocean, we may get the tsunami waves described in this book. When the plates move directly toward one another, the edge of one is forced below the edge of the other. Because of this process, called subduction, deep trenches may form. In this book we mention the deepest example, the Marianas Trench in the Pacific Ocean. When tectonic plates move apart, as they do in the Atlantic, they create large cracks in the ocean floor. Molten rock boils up through the mantle to form new floor and force the continents away from one another. The Atlantic may grow 100 feet wider in 1,000 years.

There is so much more to say! In this brief book we can only provide an introduction to this fantastic story. Here are some other books we recommend.

—-David L. Harrison

FURTHER READING

Butterfield, Moira. *Where Am I?: This Is a Watery Place; It Is Deep and Dark*. Thameside Press, 1999.

Fowler, Allan. *The Earth Is Mostly Ocean*. Children's Press (Series: Rookie-Read-About Science Series), 1995.

Kent, Peter. *Hidden Under the Sea: The World Beneath the Waves*. Dutton, 2001.

Kosek, Jane Kelly. *What's Inside the Ocean?* PowerKids Press (Series: What's Inside), 1999.

Mason, Adrienne. *Oceans: Looking at Beaches & Coral Reefs, Tides & Currents, Sea Mammals & Fish, Seaweeds & Other Ocean Wonders*. Kids Can Press, 1995.

Morris, Neil. *Oceans*. Crabtree Publishing Co. (Series: The Wonders of Our World), 1996.

Stille, Darlene. *Oceans*. Children's Press, 1999.

Svarney, Thomas E. *The Handy Ocean Answer Book*. Visible Ink Press, 2000.

Ward, Kristin. *Oceans*. PowerKids Press (Series: PowerKids Readers Nature Books), 2000.